Pandas in the Mountains

Story by Beverley Randell
Illustrations by Julian Bruére

NELSON PRICE MILBURN

Ping Ping the panda climbed
slowly up the mountainside.
She would soon give birth to a cub,
and she needed to find shelter.
When she came to an old hollow tree,
she stopped and put her head inside.

Ping Ping decided that the old tree
would be just right for a den.
She went into the forest
and broke off some leaves.
Then she carried them into the hollow
to make her den more comfortable.

Soon it started to rain,
but Ping Ping kept warm and dry
inside the hollow tree.
That night she gave birth
to a very tiny pink cub.
He was only the size of a mouse!

Ping Ping picked up her tiny baby
and fed him with her milk.
The baby had very little fur.
Ping Ping held him most of the time,
to keep him warm.

If she put him down, even for a moment,
he squealed very loudly indeed!

From now on,
Ping Ping would have to take care
of her helpless baby all the time.

When the baby was six weeks old,
he opened his eyes
and saw the bright world.
He was growing fast,
but he could not walk yet.
Ping Ping carried him in her mouth,
or tucked him under her arm,
wherever she went.

One day, Ping Ping put her baby down
while she ate some bamboo leaves.
Then she walked away
to drink at the stream.

Suddenly she sensed danger!

A wild golden cat was prowling
in the bamboo. It was hunting for rats
… or anything **else** it could find.

Ping Ping chased the golden cat away
with an angry growl.

At last, when the baby panda was three months old, he could walk. Every week, he grew bigger and braver. Soon he followed Ping Ping everywhere.

When she climbed up a tree, he would try to climb it, too. Sometimes he fell down to the ground with a bump, but he was too roly-poly to get hurt.

One cold and snowy day,
the baby panda went for a walk
by himself.
Suddenly his paws slipped!
He rolled down an icy slope.
He was not hurt,
but the ice was slippery
and he could not climb up again.

He tried to find
another way back,
but it wasn't long
before he was lost.

Ping Ping did not hear his cries
because she was making scrunching noises
as she chewed bamboo stalks.

Then she smelled something
even more delicious than bamboo.
It was roast meat!
Ping Ping followed the smell...

and she walked straight into a panda trap.
Thud! The door dropped shut behind her.

Now Ping Ping was trapped,
and her baby was alone.
She called and called to him,
but he was lost and could not
find his way back through the forest.
Ping Ping began to feel desperate.

Then Ping Ping heard some people coming.
Suddenly she felt a sting in her shoulder!
A dart had hit her,
and very soon it sent her to sleep.

While Ping Ping was asleep,
the vets who had fired the dart gun
fitted a collar around her neck.
A small radio transmitter on the collar
would send out signals
to help them track her.

When Ping Ping woke up she was free again.
She moved off quickly to search for her baby.
She had been away from him
for much too long.
There were dangerous animals in the forest.
Wild cats, leopards, foxes and wolves
would all eat a baby panda if they could.

Ping Ping had to find him before they did!

At last, Ping Ping scented him on the wind, and hurried down the mountainside to reach him.

There he was—safe and sound.
He ran to her and she cuddled him tightly.
She fed him and kept him in her arms.

The vets who had been following her
were excited when they saw the baby.
They knew that the survival
of every panda cub was important.
They named him Lin Lin, which means Forest.

And there in the forest
Lin Lin stayed with his mother,
and went on growing and learning.
Ping Ping showed him all the best places
to find bamboo, and where to drink
and where to rest.

At last, when he was two years old,
he was as big as his mother,
and he knew how to take care of himself.

Lin Lin, the baby panda, had grown up.